Sarah Watts

Ready, Steady Recorder!

kevin mayhew

kevin
mayhew

First published in Great Britain in 2013
by Kevin Mayhew Ltd.
Buxhall, Stowmarket, Suffolk IP14 3BW
Tel: +44 (0) 1449 737978
E-mail: info@kevinmayhew.com

www.kevinmayhew.com

9 8 7 6 5 4 3

Pupil Book
ISBN 978 1 84867 591 9
ISMN M 57042 206 7
Catalogue No. 3612501

Pupil Classroom Pack
(10 pupil books with 1 Audio CD)
Catalogue No. 3612502

Cover design: Rob Mortonson.
© Images used under licence from Shutterstock Inc.
Music editor: Donald Thomson
Proofread by: Marian Hellen

Printed and bound in Great Britain

Thank you to Jackey Birch for
good advice and encouragement

All of Sarah's music may be viewed at
www.kevinmayhew.com
and Sarah's own website is at www.sarah-watts.com

Scan the QR code with your smart phone to see her books on www.kevinmayhew.com

Ready, Steady Recorder! is a colourful recorder tutor for early starters.

Introducing the notes slowly and clearly, it teaches good technique and musical literacy with humour and fun.

There are plenty of short pieces with jazzy piano or CD accompaniments at all stages. Many have funny words or actions to aid learning. There is even a fanfare to play as each note is taught, and a chance to take a bow!

Rhythm rhymes, movement, performance ideas and opportunities to play by ear make playing the recorder in the early stages even more fun!

I hope you enjoy it!

Key to symbols

Clap the rhythm and say the fun rhyme to reinforce note and rhythm learning

A fanfare to celebrate achievement as each note is learned

A call and response game, played to a jazzy CD accompaniment

A few ideas to make learning the recorder even more fun!

An easy explanation of musical terms and symbols

A few playing technique reminders along the way

Contents

First, listen to
The Grand Recorder March…

TRACK
1

Clap or move to the music

Now let's play!

This is how to hold your recorder

Your left hand MUST go at the top (even if you are left-handed).
The left thumb will cover the back hole, and the right thumb
will support the back of the recorder behind the 4th hole.

First practise whispering **du**. This is called tonguing.

Put the tip of the recorder mouthpiece between your lips (don't let it touch your teeth).

Breathe in through your mouth and blow gently into the recorder – starting the note with a **du**
(don't blow too hard or you will squeak).

Listen and make the note as nice as possible.

Don't Forget! Always start a note with a **du**.

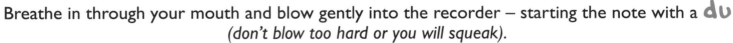

This is how to play B

Gently does it!

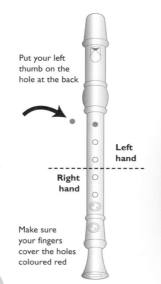

Put your left thumb on the hole at the back

Left hand

Right hand

Make sure your fingers cover the holes coloured red

AFTER ME!

TRACK 2

First listen, then play the notes

WHAT'S THIS?

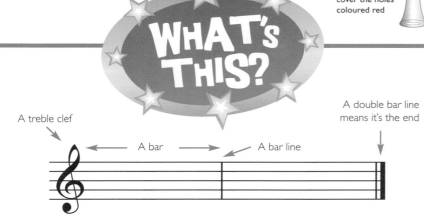

A treble clef

← A bar →

A bar line

A double bar line means it's the end

This is a STAVE ... the notes are written on here

This is a
ONE BEAT NOTE
– it's called a crotchet

This is a
ONE BEAT REST

This tells you there are four beats in a bar,

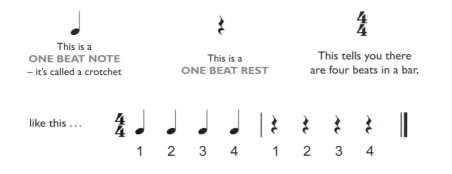

like this ...

1   2   3   4   1   2   3   4

8

1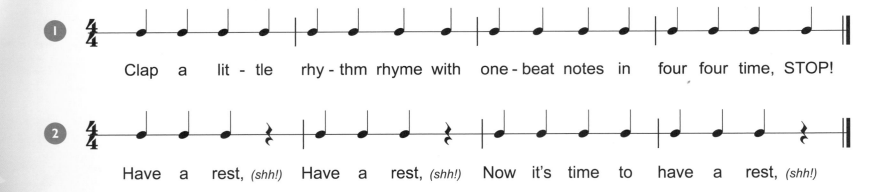

Clap   a   lit - tle   rhy - thm rhyme with   one - beat notes in   four four time, STOP!

2

Have   a   rest, *(shh!)* Have   a   rest, *(shh!)* Now it's time to have a   rest, *(shh!)*

This is where B goes on the music

Play these B's.

Fin - ger, thumb,   let's play B.   Count the lines, it's   one, two, three.

Here's A

This is where it goes on the music

Put your left
thumb on the
hole at the back

**Left
hand**

**Right
hand**

Make sure
your fingers
cover the holes
coloured red

Play these A's

Down to A, fin - gers two, se - cond space and whis - per du.

AFTER ME!

TRACK 8

First listen, then play the notes

WHAT'S THIS?

♩ This is a **TWO BEAT NOTE** – it's called a minim (count 1, 2)

▬ This is a **TWO BEAT REST** (it sits on the line)

p (piano) Play softly

f (forte) Play loudly

Count: 1 2 3 4 1 2 3 4

Clap and say these RHYTHM RHYMES

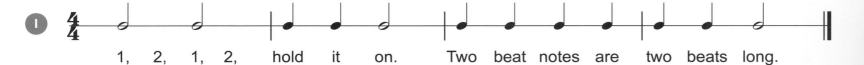

1 1, 2, 1, 2, hold it on. Two beat notes are two beats long.

2 Have a rest for two beats *(shh! shh!)* Two beats *(shh! shh!)* Two beats *(shh! shh!)*

⭐ What's The Time? Ten To Three ⭐

TRACK 9 PRACTICE   TRACK 10 PERFORMANCE

Play twice

What's the time? Ten to three. Don't for-get to play A B.

Play twice or sing the second time

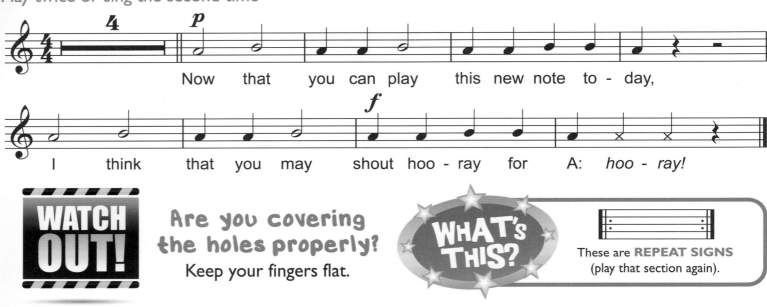

Now that you can play this new note to-day,
I think that you may shout hoo-ray for A: *hoo-ray!*

WATCH OUT! Are you covering the holes properly? Keep your fingers flat.

WHAT'S THIS? These are **REPEAT SIGNS** (play that section again).

Walking pace

Walk-ing round to the beat, feel the mu-sic in your feet.
If you like to walk a lot, you can do it on the spot.

Second time: sing and walk in time to the music either around the room or on the spot.

Here's G

This is where it goes on the music

Play these G's

Put your left thumb on the hole at the back

Left hand

Right hand

Make sure your fingers cover the holes coloured red

Now it's G, fin - gers three, se - cond line, count care - ful - ly.

AFTER ME!

TRACK 19

First listen, then play the notes

WATCH OUT!

Are you still tonguing?
Always start the note with a **du**
(very important).

WHAT'S THIS?

○ This is **FOUR BEAT NOTE** – it's called a SEMIBREVE (count 1, 2, 3, 4).

Count: 1   2   3   4

▬ This is a **WHOLE BAR REST** (it hangs from the line).

Count: 1   2   3   4

mf (mezzo forte) Medium loud   *mp* (mezzo piano) Medium soft

Clap and say these **RHYTHM RHYMES**

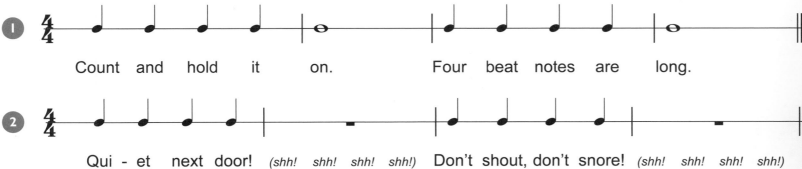

1 Count and hold it on.   Four beat notes are long.

2 Qui - et next door! *(shh! shh! shh! shh!)* Don't shout, don't snore! *(shh! shh! shh! shh!)*

 Ready, Steady, G!

PRACTICE PERFORMANCE

Rea - dy, stea - dy, 1 2 3 4. Let's get rea - dy, 1 2 3 4.

Count to four and play with me, rea - dy, stea - dy, G!

Don't forget to breathe in through your mouth before you play.
Find good places in the music to take new breaths.

 Barefoot Boogie

PRACTICE PERFORMANCE

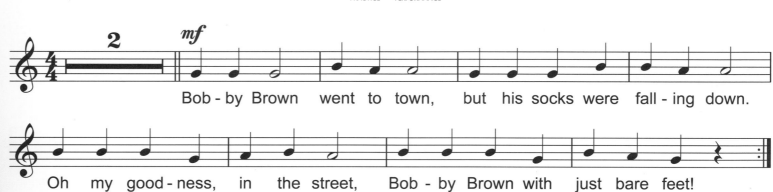

Bob - by Brown went to town, but his socks were fall - ing down.

Oh my good - ness, in the street, Bob - by Brown with just bare feet!

This is a **HALF BEAT NOTE** – it's called a quaver.

Two of them together make one beat.

Count: 1 and 2 and 3 and 4 and

Are you blowing gently?
. . . remember blowing bubbles? . . . don't let them pop.
Are you making a really nice sound?

PRACTICE   PERFORMANCE

Sing second time through!

I bet you ne - ver knew, I could play this piece to you.

2nd time: put your arms out and pose like a star!

Don't you think I am a star for get - ting this far? *Ta dah!*

 **Stop And Hop**

TRACK 26 PRACTICE TRACK 27 PERFORMANCE

This piece is fun, **but don't forget to take your recorder right out of your mouth before you hop!** Keep your fingers over the holes ready to play again.

Tango

mf

Hop, hop, hop, hop, hop, hop, hop!

Hop, hop, hop, hop, hop, hop, hop!

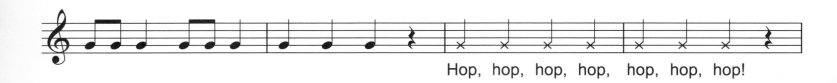

Hop, hop, hop, hop, hop, hop, hop!

Don't hop!   Jump!

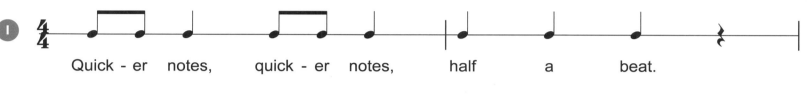

Quick - er notes, quick - er notes, half a beat.

Run - ning, run - ning, run - ning, run - ning down the street.

1

Why not...

Make a Wall of Fame!

Draw a picture of you and your recorder, and put it on the wall.

TAKE A BOW!

Now that you can play **G**, play the **Take a Bow Fanfare**

TRACK 7

and take a bow!

Introducing E

This is where it goes on the music

Play these E's

Put your left thumb on the hole at the back

Left hand

Right hand

Make sure your fingers cover the holes coloured red

AFTER ME!

First listen, then play the notes

Two more fin-gers down we climb, E is on the bot-tom line.

New Note E, You Don't Scare Me!

TRACK 29 PRACTICE

TRACK 30 PERFORMANCE

TRACK 28

4 *mf*

E G E E G E E G G B B B.

E G E E G, new note E, you don't scare me!

 **Look! Two Hands!**

TRACK 31 PRACTICE   TRACK 32 PERFORMANCE

Charleston

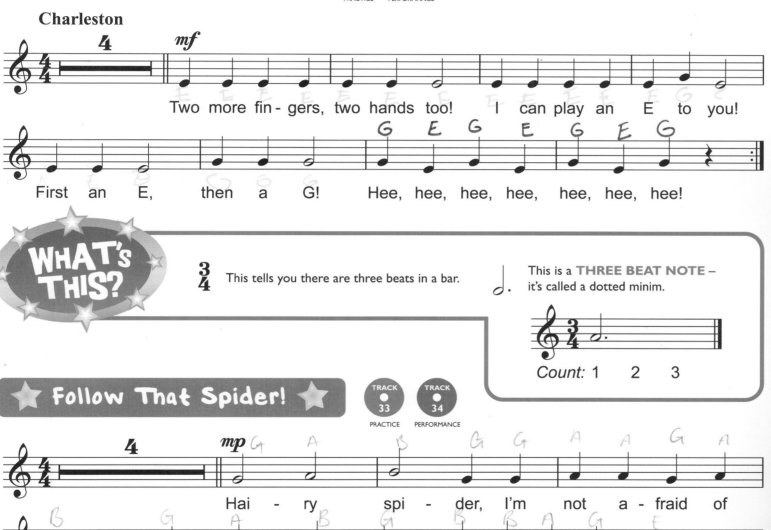

Two more fin - gers, two hands too! I can play an E to you!

First an E, then a G! Hee, hee, hee, hee, hee, hee, hee!

WHAT'S THIS?

$\frac{3}{4}$ This tells you there are three beats in a bar.

This is a **THREE BEAT NOTE** – it's called a dotted minim.

Count: 1   2   3

Follow That Spider!

TRACK 33 PRACTICE   TRACK 34 PERFORMANCE

Hai - ry spi - der, I'm not a - fraid of

you. Just look cree - py, that's all you can do!

TRACK 35 PRACTICE
TRACK 36 PERFORMANCE

When you're stand-ing in a queue, there is some-thing you can do. Please re-mem-ber how to play, E E E E B and A.

Clap and say these **RHYTHM RHYMES**

WATCH OUT!

Never hold the recorder with one hand when you are playing.

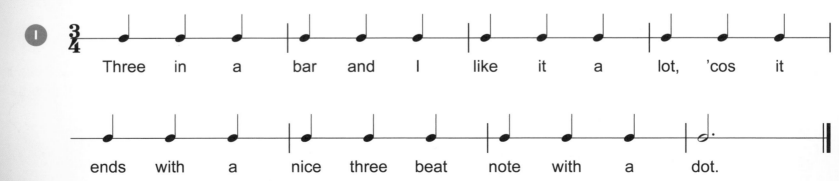

Three in a bar and I like it a lot, 'cos it ends with a nice three beat note with a dot.

⭐ The Dotty Waltz ⭐

PRACTICE   PERFORMANCE

Why not...
Play to yourself
in the mirror?

Are you standing straight?

TAKE A BOW!

Now that you can play **E**, play the **Take a Bow Fanfare**

TRACK 7

and take a bow!

Here's low D

This is where it goes on the music

Play these low D's

AFTER ME!

One more fin - ger, gen - tly blow. Down to D and get - ting low.

⭐ **Not On Your Head!** ⭐

TRACK 40 PRACTICE

TRACK 41 PERFORMANCE

Light rock feel

mf

Play your re - cor - der a - ny time, at break - fast or in

bed. But I think it might be dif - fi - cult while stand - ing on your head!

TRACK 39

First listen, then play the notes

Put your left thumb on the hole at the back

Left hand

Right hand

Make sure your fingers cover the holes coloured red

 Smelly Cheese

TRACK 42 PRACTICE TRACK 43 PERFORMANCE

Smel - ly, smel - ly, smel - ly cheese, tastes so good, but

watch out please. If it starts to real - ly pong, you have kept it far too long.

 Play A Recorder!

TRACK 44 PRACTICE TRACK 45 PERFORMANCE

If you're feel - ing sad and blue and you don't know what to do,

Sing:

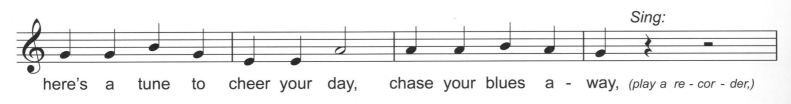

here's a tune to cheer your day, chase your blues a - way, *(play a re - cor - der,)*

Sing:

chase your blues a - way, *(play a re - cor - der,)* chase your blues a - way.

⭐ **Just Checking** ⭐

TRACK 46 — PRACTICE TRACK 47 — PERFORMANCE

mf

Play re - cor- der, O K, stop!   Is your left hand at the top?

Clap and say these
RHYTHM RHYMES

Clap this three times, getting faster each time

1

I'm gon-na clap a   rhy-thm rhyme.   Shall I clap it   one more time? *Yes!*
Yes!
No!

Now that you can play low D, play the **Take a Bow Fanfare**

TRACK 7

and take a bow!

Why not...
Practise recorder notes with your recorder on your chin instead of in your mouth?

(Especially good if you've been asked to be quiet!)

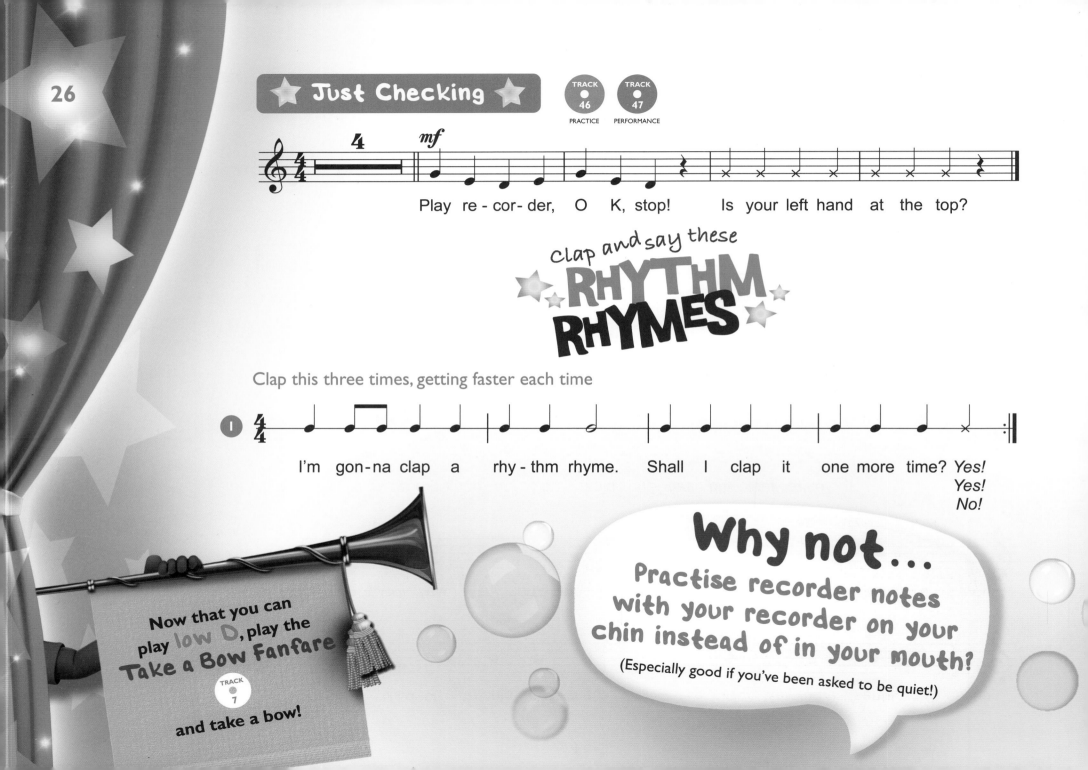

And now C

This is where it goes on the music

Play these C's

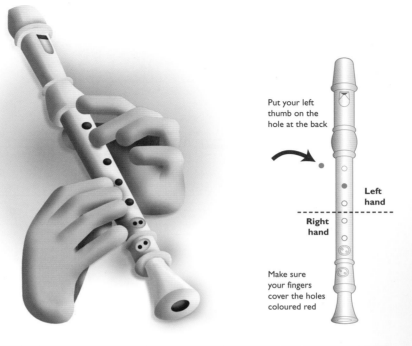

Put your left thumb on the hole at the back

Left hand

Right hand

Make sure your fingers cover the holes coloured red

Mid - dle fin - ger and a thumb. Third space C, now up we come.

⭐ **Just Like That!** ⭐

TRACK ● 49 PRACTICE TRACK ● 50 PERFORMANCE

With razzle dazzle!

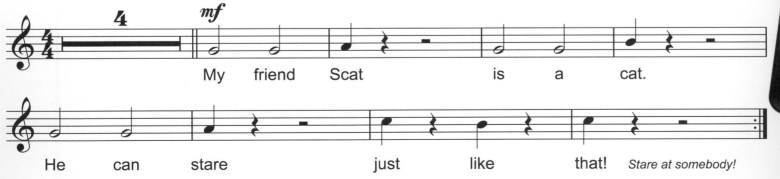

mf

My friend Scat is a cat.

He can stare just like that! *Stare at somebody!*

AFTER ME!

TRACK ● 48

First listen, then play the notes

Thoughts And Dreams

TRACK ● 51 PRACTICE
TRACK ● 52 PERFORMANCE

Slow

p

WHAT'S THIS?

(Staccato) A dot over or under a note tells you to play it really short.

This means **PAUSE** (stay on the note a bit longer).

How Do You Do?

TRACK ● 53 PRACTICE
TRACK ● 54 PERFORMANCE

Rock feel

mf

Hey, good morn - ing, how do you do?

I'm al - right thanks, hope you are too. I'm ve - ry well thanks,

can't tell a lie. That's O K then, good - bye!

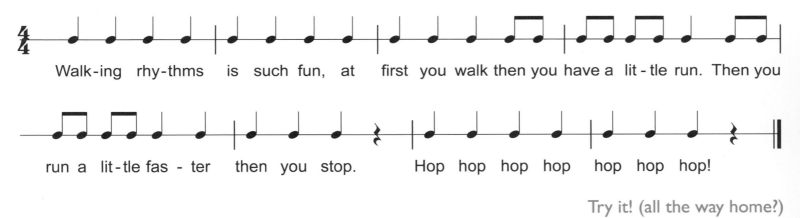

Walk-ing rhy-thms is such fun, at first you walk then you have a lit-tle run. Then you

run a lit-tle fas-ter then you stop. Hop hop hop hop hop hop hop!

Try it! (all the way home?)

 **Odd Sock Samba**

TRACK
55
PRACTICE

TRACK
56
PERFORMANCE

With a latin feel

mf

WATCH OUT!

Sit up or stand straight when you play.
(This will help you breathe.)

⭐ Who's That? ⭐

TRACK 57 PRACTICE   TRACK 58 PERFORMANCE

mf

Who's that knock-ing at   my front door?   Yes, it's some-one I've

seen be-fore.   I can see that it's my friend Jim. *(knock on the ta-ble)*   Come in!

Now that you can play **C**, play the **Take a Bow Fanfare**

TRACK 7

and take a bow!

Why not...
Have a parade!
and play your favourite recorder tune.

Now high D

This is where it goes on the music

Play these high D's

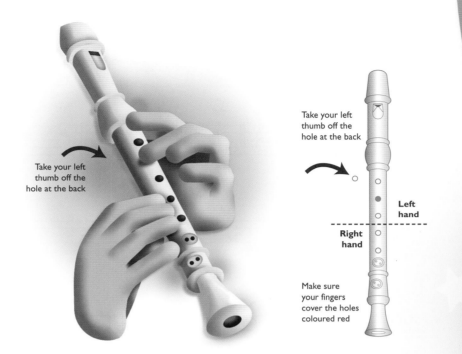

Take your left thumb off the hole at the back

Take your left thumb off the hole at the back

Left hand

Right hand

Make sure your fingers cover the holes coloured red

High D sit - ting on line four, look - ing down at C next door.

WHAT'S THIS?

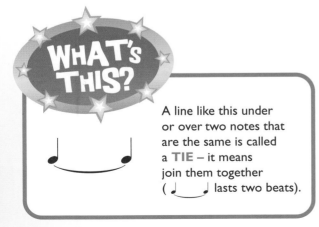

A line like this under or over two notes that are the same is called a **TIE** – it means join them together (♩___♩ lasts two beats).

WATCH OUT!

Keep your recorder clean and dry.

AFTER ME!

TRACK 59

First listen, then play the notes

Funnybone Boogie

TRACK 60 PRACTICE TRACK 61 PERFORMANCE

Howdy, High D

TRACK 62 PRACTICE TRACK 63 PERFORMANCE

High D, high D, high D D.   High D, how d'you do?

High D, high D, high D D, a ve - ry good day to you.

Clap and say these RHYTHM RHYMES

 Ties like this will join notes up, join notes up, join notes up.

The Chummy Charleston

 TRACK 64 PRACTICE TRACK 65 PERFORMANCE

With a swing

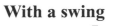

Why not...
Do a Concert?
Show everyone how well you are doing.

TAKE A BOW!

Now that you can play high D, play the **Take a Bow Fanfare**

TRACK 7

and take a bow!

And next F sharp

This is where it goes on the music

Play these F sharps

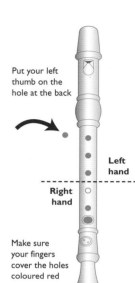

Put your left thumb on the hole at the back

Left hand

Right hand

Make sure your fingers cover the holes coloured red

Here's F sharp, and you will see a sharp at the start to tell you the key.

AFTER ME!

TRACK 66

First listen, then play the notes

WHAT'S THIS?

— A **SHARP** makes a note a semitone (half a note) higher

This tells you all the F's in the piece will be F sharps (it's called a key signature).

legato   play smoothly

A line above or below two or more notes that are different is a **SLUR**. Tongue the first note and join the rest smoothly together.

 September Saz

TRACK 67 PRACTICE

TRACK 68 PERFORMANCE

mp *legato*

Are you listening when you play?

Listen to yourself, the accompaniment,
and other people who are playing.

 Proud Moment

TRACK 69 PRACTICE

TRACK 70 PERFORMANCE

Grandly

I'd   like you   all   to know   I can play F sharp, and so

2nd time:
pose in a proud sort of way!

I   would like   it   un - der - stood I'm   get - ting   quite   good!

Now C sharp

This is where it goes on the music

Play these C sharps

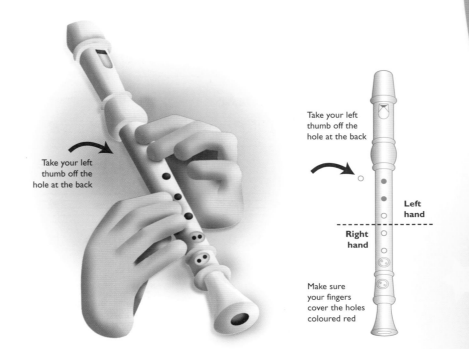

Take your left thumb off the hole at the back

Take your left thumb off the hole at the back

Left hand

Right hand

Make sure your fingers cover the holes coloured red

Just two fin - gers and no thumb. Watch out, C sharp here I come!

WHAT'S THIS?

This key signature tells you there are two sharps in the piece (F♯ and C♯).

A **NATURAL SIGN** means play the normal note, not the sharp (as we haven't done flats yet).

AFTER ME!

TRACK 75

First listen, then play the notes

Look, No Thumb!

TRACK 76 PRACTICE   TRACK 77 PERFORMANCE

mf

I be-lieve two-note tunes aren't so good to hum.

What is good a - bout this piece is you don't need your thumb.

clap and say these RHYTHM RHYMES

WHAT'S THIS?

This is a dotted quaver and a semiquaver pattern. It fits into one beat.

Count: 1   2   3   4

1

Skip a dot-ted rhy-thm when you're skip-ping down the street.

1   2   3   4   skip - ping to the beat.

Hey! Mr May

TRACK 78 — PRACTICE
TRACK 79 — PERFORMANCE

Woo Hoo! - Get You

TRACK 80 — PRACTICE
TRACK 81 — PERFORMANCE

Woo!

Why not...

Play your recorder with other people in a group or a band?

TAKE A BOW!

Now that you can play C sharp, play the **Take a Bow Fanfare**

TRACK 7

and take a bow!

And finally F

This is where it goes on the music

Play these F's

Put your left thumb on the hole at the back

Left hand

Right hand

Make sure your fingers cover the holes coloured red

AFTER ME!

Just plain F   in the bot - tom space.   Last note   in the book, smi - ley   face!

TRACK 82

First listen, then play the notes

WHAT'S THIS?

♩. A dot makes a note last half as long again, so a dotted crochet lasts for 1 ½ beats.

Practise clapping these rhythms

These sound the same

1

Count: 1   2 & 3

2

Count: 1   2 & 3

3

Count: 1   2 & 3

Clap and say these RHYTHM RHYMES

1

Skip - ping round but skip - ping slow can show how dot - ted rhy - thms go.

 Boating Lake Lullaby

 TRACK 83 PRACTICE

 TRACK 84 PERFORMANCE

Gliding

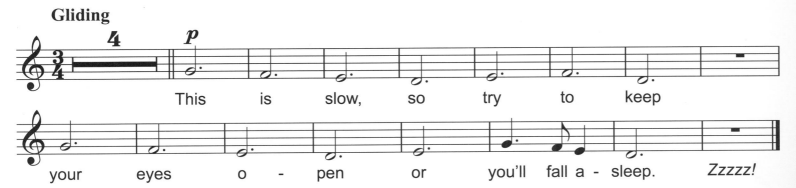

This   is   slow,   so   try   to   keep

your   eyes   o - pen   or   you'll   fall a - sleep.   *Zzzzz!*

Make sure your little finger is
ALWAYS down when you play an F.

⭐ Little Finger Fun ⭐

TRACK 85 — PRACTICE TRACK 86 — PERFORMANCE

Can you play E to-day? Then an F to E? Is your

lit - tle fin - ger down for F? Have a look and see.

You are getting very good now, but make sure you are still tonguing the beginning of each note, and holding your recorder properly.

⭐ Mrs Shrimp Soon Found Out ⭐

TRACK 87 — PRACTICE TRACK 88 — PERFORMANCE

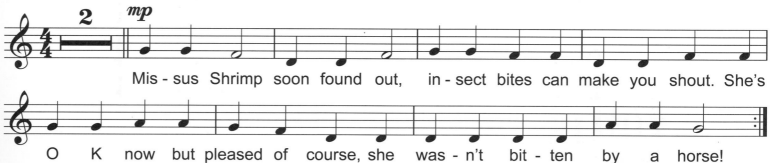

Mis - sus Shrimp soon found out, in - sect bites can make you shout. She's

O K now but pleased of course, she was - n't bit - ten by a horse!

 **I Did It!**

 TRACK 89 PRACTICE   TRACK 90 PERFORMANCE

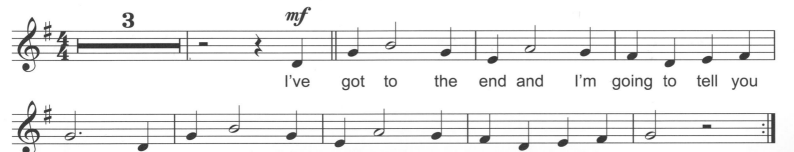

I've got to the end and I'm going to tell you how. I worked ve - ry hard and I'm going to take a bow!

 **Ready, Steady Recorder!**

Why not...
Find out more about the recorder now?

There is some lovely music to play going back hundreds of years.

The most important thing to do is **have fun!**

TAKE A BOW!

Now that you can play **F** and have finished the book, play the **Take a Bow Fanfare**

 TRACK 7

and take a bow!